D0678720

THE OPEN MEDIA PAMPHLET SERIES

THE OPEN MEDIA PAMPHLET SERIES

against war in iraq

an anti-war primer

MICHAEL RATNER
JENNIE GREEN
BARBARA OLSHANSKY
of the
CENTER FOR CONSTITUTIONAL RIGHTS

Series Editor Greg Ruggiero

SEVEN STORIES PRESS / NEW YORK

A Seven Stories Press First Edition.

ISBN: 1-58322-591-9

Cover design by Greg Ruggiero.

Front cover photo: U.S. Marines patrol the perimeter at
    Camp Commando in Kuwait, December 2, 2002. The
    Marines have set up a command headquarters for the 1st
    Marine Expeditionary Force in preparation for "further
    developments in the region. (Joe Raedle/Getty Images)

Back cover photo: U.S. troops keep their weapons close dur-
    ing Thanksgiving dinner November 28, 2002 at Bagram
    airbase in Afghanistan. (Scott Nelson/Getty Images)

Printed in Canada

9 8 7 6 5 4 3 2 1

"Let it not be said that people in the United States did nothing when their government declared a war without limit and instituted stark new measures of repression…"

—FROM "NOT IN OUR NAME" STATEMENT OF CONSCIENCE AGAINST WAR WITH IRAQ

THE BUSH ADMINISTRATION IS taking us on a dizzying ride toward a war with Iraq. An American attack against Iraq is not justified by any imminent threat to the United States nor does it have the backing of the United Nations Security Council. An American war against Iraq without explicit authority from the United Nations is flatly illegal.

This pamphlet details some of the Bush Administration's alleged justifications for a new war against Iraq, as well as the legal violations, underlying motives, consequences, and alternatives.

The Administration has presented a large amount of confusing information, but has not given any persuasive factual basis justifying a war. Its "facts" about Iraqi weapons of mass destruction and complicity in terrorism are exaggerated, misleading, or false. They are contrary to the findings of the weapons inspectors who have actually examined Iraq's capabilities. To the extent there are unknown facts, the ongoing inspections will give us answers.

The U.S. push toward war with Iraq stems from longer-term political and economic goals: in particular, control of the state with the second largest oil reserves in the world and the domination of the Middle East, which possesses the world's largest supply of oil. The United States, as the unchallenged superpower, is redrawing the map of the world in a fashion that will continue its hegemony for many years. First, it did so in Central Asia (another oil-rich area), and now it is doing so in the Middle East.

To insure U.S. domination by military means, the Bush Administration is putting forth a new doctrine. That doctrine, formally released to the public on September 20, 2002, asserts that the U.S. can employ "pre-emptive strikes" even if there are no immediate threats. Such strikes would violate the terms of the U.N. Charter and a fundamental principle of international law—the prohibition of aggressive war.

Nor do any U.N. resolutions justify force against Iraq. Despite U.S. statements to the contrary, the most recent Security Council resolution, 1441, passed on November 8, 2002, states that the current weapons inspectors are to report their findings to the Security Council. It will then be up to the Security Council, and not individual countries, to determine what next steps might be taken regarding Iraq. These could include options ranging from lifting the embargo to authorizing the use of violence.

There are alternatives to war. Reliance upon the U.N is crucial. The inspections have hopefully delayed the war and they continue to be a good alternative. The fear, of course, is that the United States will deem violations, even minor ones, as a pretext for war. The alternative is the United Nations and reliance on international law. The goal—to make the world safer—is to strengthen the United Nations and international law. We all must work for disarmament—either universal disarmament or at least a Weapons-of-Mass-Destruction–Free Zone in the Middle East.

The dire consequences of this war are breathtaking. American casualties could be in the thousands; Iraqi casualties could be in excess of 200,000. In the United States, communities of color will disproportionately suffer these deaths and injuries. An American war with Iraq poses a serious threat to the Middle East, an area whose volatility is already acute. A war is surely going to increase terrorism around the world—something the Bush Administration is acknowledging by calling up 265,000 reservists and National Guard members to protect us at home from the intensified threat. The money we spend on war will not be spent at home where it is needed at this time of economic decline. The Administration is relying on the power of violence rather than the rule of law and respect for human rights. As a result, everyone will be less safe.

The time is now to protest and prevent the spiral toward increased militarism and war. It is not a time for silence, but a time to protest—and protest loudly.

I. IS THERE A NEED FOR WAR?

Just how much do we need to be concerned about Iraq's threats to our security and to world peace? Is there hard evidence of such threats, and if so, what is this evidence? Why is the issue of threats from Iraq being raised now; how urgent and immediate is the problem?

Our initial question must be whether there is evidence of an Iraqi policy that targets Americans or the United States, or presents a serious threat to any of our neighbors. In truth, the Iraqi regime led by Saddam Hussein has never targeted the United States or any other Western power.

However, Iraq certainly has been a threat to its own neighbors, and Saddam Hussein has attacked Kurds living inside Iraq as well. The invasions of Iran and Kuwait, the bombing of Israel, and the bitter suppression of the Kurdish people in the 1980s attest to the existence of a regime that has consistently been willing to violate human rights and state sovereignty.[1]

In order to evaluate any risks that other countries may currently face from Iraq, we must examine the circumstances under which those attacks took place. A great deal of the current controversy has focused on Iraq's use of "weapons of mass destruction" (WMD), a phrase interpreted as including nuclear, chemical, and biological weapons. The Iraqi regime's use of chemical weapons in its internal campaign against the Kurds in 1988 was not condemned by the United States or Britain. Instead, both countries increased their financial aid to Iraq during that time in order to assist Iraq in its efforts against Iran.

The Iraqi government's only use of chemical weapons outside its borders occurred during its war on Iran from 1981 through 1988.[2] The use of chemical agents during that war was undertaken with the complicity of both the United States and Britain. The United States confirmed the use of such weapons in 1983—as did the United Nations in 1984—and yet it continued to provide Iraq with helicopters that would be used in the chemical attacks, to give Iraq access to critical intelligence information, to lend technical assistance in the form of air force personnel, and then blocked condemnation of Iraq's chemical weapons attacks at the U.N. Security Council. In short, Iraq has never used chemical weapons against an external enemy without the acquiescence of the United States. The same can be said for Iraq's internal use of such weapons.

The other currently hypothesized threat to the West—that Iraq plans to supply terrorist organizations with weapons of mass destruction, a prospect raised by the Bush Administration in early 2002— is wholly unsubstantiated. The two paramilitary groups that the Iraqi regime currently supports, the Mujahedin I-Khalq and the Arab Liberation Front, have no access to advanced unconventional weaponry from the government, and have never carried out attacks in the United States or Europe.[3]

Similarly, there is no evidence linking Saddam Hussein's regime to Al Qaeda's terrorist network. Hussein's political party, the Ba'ath party, is secular in orientation and strongly opposed to fundamentalism and the radical religious currents from which followers of Osama bin Laden have been drawn. Al Qaeda, on the other hand, openly professes that one of its missions is to overthrow secular governments and replace them with Islamic regimes. The threat to his own rule from groups like Al Qaeda thus makes any anti-U.S. collaboration between Hussein's regime and Al Qaeda highly unlikely.

There is simply no proof of any political relationship between Iraq and Al Qaeda, despite persistent efforts by the United States and others to uncover one. The dossier released by the British government on September 24, 2002, presented no evidence of any Al Qaeda–Iraq links. Promises by U.S. officials, including Secretary of Defense Donald Rumsfeld, National Security Advisor Condoleezza Rice, and others, that hard evidence of such links would be provided have gone completely unfulfilled.[4] No U.S. intelligence agency including the CIA or the DIA has established such a link. In the aftermath of 9/11, the U.S. charged that an Iraqi diplomat and an Al Qaeda operative met in the Czech republic—but the charge was false, as was recently stated by Czech president Vaclav Havel. Now, in desperation, Rumsfeld has set up his own intelligence group to look for such links.

It is difficult to imagine the circumstances in which Iraq would use chemical, biological, or nuclear weapons against any Western country, given the massive reprisals that it would face. The only conceivable scenario would be one in which Saddam Hussein felt that the country had nothing to lose because it was faced with its imminent demise. Under these conditions, it seems that America's best way of avoiding such a doomsday scenario would be to use methods other than military violence to address political concerns.

Is There Evidence That Iraq Has Weapons of Mass Destruction?

Even if Iraq has intentions of targeting the United States and/or other countries, what evidence do we have of Iraq's capability of carrying out such a threat?

Despite the pervasive use of the phrase "weapons of mass destruction" in many of the Bush Administration's speeches discussing Saddam Hussein throughout 2002, there is no evidence of a developed nuclear weapons program in Iraq. Indeed, all reliable, detailed evidence from independent experts[5] reveals that the current weapons capacity in Iraq is small—smaller and far less advanced than that of other countries around the world that are actively threatening peace in their respective regions.

Analysts from all political backgrounds agree that Saddam Hussein's military position is far weaker today than it was before the 1991 Gulf War—a war in which his armies were decisively defeated.[6] The 1991 war was extremely destructive and has been followed by more than a decade of devastating sanctions which surely have reduced the country's capacity for war-making.[7] Furthermore, Iraq's arsenal and military powers have remained suppressed, experts note, due to the country's lack of arms imports and the use of "no-fly zones" (airspace over parts of Iraq from which Iraqi airplanes are excluded), overflights, intensive surveillance, and persistent bombing by American and British forces.[8]

In 2002 alone, the United States and Britain bombed Iraq more than forty-six times, allegedly because of Iraqi attacks from within the no-fly zones. The United States and Britain, by creating these no-fly zones and using military force to police them, have unequivocally violated the United Nations Charter.[9]

The U.N. Special Commission (UNSCOM) charged with the responsibility of verifying Iraq's compliance with the weapons provisions of U.N. Security Council Resolution 687 (recognizing the ceasefire of the 1991 Gulf War) first entered Iraq in 1991. UNSCOM along with the International Atomic Energy Agency (IAEA) continued their work there until December 1998. Reports filed by UNSCOM after it left Iraq documented that 817 of Iraq's 819 Soviet-built ballistic missiles, the country's long-range delivery system, had been located and destroyed. In addition, the IAEA inspected and, with the compliance of the Iraqi regime, destroyed all of the country's facilities capable of producing material for a nuclear weapons program. In its report to the U.N. Security Council on October 8, 1997, the IAEA stated that Iraq had compiled a "full, final, and complete" account of all of its nuclear projects. The Agency found no indication of any prohibited activities. In a follow-up report, issued on April 25, 2002, the IAEA further stated that "[t]here were no indications that there remains in Iraq any physical capability for the production of amounts of weapons-usable nuclear material of any practical significance."[10]

Analysts are also clear that after the inspections, Iraq retained no operating uranium extraction facilities.[11] Moreover, because the process of enriching uranium for use in nuclear weapons systems requires a substantial infrastructure and power supply—facilities that can easily be spotted during American and British flyovers—there is no basis to believe that Iraq possesses this critical ingredient for a nuclear arsenal.[12] The absence of such evidence weighs heavily in favor of inspections; we cannot know what Iraq is planning without undertaking an investigation. In making its case for war, the Bush Administration has presumed the outcome of such inspections.

Administration officials have referred as well to photos that "reveal that the regime is rebuilding facilities that it has used to produce chemical and biological weapons."[13] The major facilities that Iraq used to produce chemical warfare agents was destroyed partially through bombardment and partially by UNSCOM action. Iraq's main biological weapons facility was destroyed in the summer of 1996.[14] In addition to being unverifiable in the absence of inspections, there is no information available to prove or disprove the contention that these facilities are being rebuilt or to indicate how such facilities are being used.

Concerns about Iraq's chemical and biological weapons stockpile seem hypothesized or exaggerated as well. To be sure, Iraq has never provided a full declaration describing its use of these weapons during its war against Iran, nor has it provided sufficient proof of its destruction of large quantities of its stocks. However, it is clear that much of the previously developed stock has deteriorated beyond use. A January 1998 report from UNSCOM notes that, "Taking into consideration the conditions and the quality of chemical weapons agents and munitions produced by Iraq at that time, there is no possibility of weapons remaining from the mid-1980s."[15] Professor Anthony Cordesman of the Center for Strategic and International Studies has reached similar conclusions about Iraq's biological weapons: "The shelf-life and lethality of Iraq's weapons is unknown, but it seems likely that the shelf-life was limited. In balance, it seems probable that any agents Iraq retained after the Gulf War now have very limited lethality, if any."[16]

Weapons experts agree that there are two potential exceptions to the deterioration process: mustard gas and VX nerve agent. However, even these provide no present cause for concern. UNSCOM witnessed and supervised the destruction of 12,747 of Iraq's 13,500 mustard gas shells during the seven-year inspection period. While there is no way to verify the Iraqi government's claim that the remaining shells were destroyed by the British and American bombardments, former U.N. weapons inspector Scott Ritter notes that such a limited number of shells have "little military value on the modern battlefield."[17] While the nerve agent VX also would not deteriorate significantly over time, UNSCOM investigations made it clear that Iraq did not have the advanced technology necessary to produce such a weapon on a large scale, and the limited equipment that the country did have was destroyed in 1996. Further, UNSCOM's tests indicated that the equipment had never been used.

Obviously, as the inspectors have not been back to Iraq for four years, it is unknown what weapons of mass destruction Iraq is working toward or now possesses. However, it is not speculation, based upon what is known, to state that Iraq has no nuclear weapons and no means to deliver weapons of mass destruction at any great distance. Nor is there any chance it will have nuclear weapons in the foreseeable future. Although Iraq may have some chemical and biological weapons, these can be ferreted out with inspections; a full-scale war is hardly necessary to eradicate them. It should also be remembered that although Iraq possessed such weapons in the 1991 war, it did not use them, probably due to its knowledge that if it did, the United States would have gone on to Baghdad.

Perhaps most significant in this analysis, however, is the fact that even if Iraq had retained viable chemical or biological weapons and was inclined to use them, it still would not present a threat to another country. Without a missile system capable of delivering such an attack, Iraq poses no threat. Even the strongest proponents of an invasion of Iraq admit that Iraq's arsenal holds only twelve to fourteen missiles, not nearly enough to launch an attack.[18] Furthermore, biological weapons cannot be disbursed through ballistic missiles, and the contention recently stated by President Bush—that Iraq may have developed an unmanned aerial vehicle to deliver such weapons to the United States undetected—is, according to experts, entirely untenable.[19]

The likelihood of Saddam Hussein using such weapons, if Iraq even possesses them, is clearly much greater if the United States begins an unprovoked war against Iraq. As the CIA confirmed in its recent report to Congress, if Saddam Hussein has nothing to lose, the chances are greater that he will attack. The report also states that there presently is no threat of attack from Iraq.[20]

So it appears that the Bush Administration's war is not about responding to an armed attack upon the United States or one of our allies; it is not about anticipatory self-defense, as no attack is imminent; it is not about a pre-emptive strike, as there is nothing to preempt. At best it would be an attack because of speculation that at some point in the future Iraq might constitute a danger. That is hardly the stuff of war, particularly when inspections can address any immediate problems of weapons of mass destruction.

Why Start a War?

Given the Bush Administration's push for war with Iraq, it is important to look behind the rhetoric and try to understand the practical politics involved.

There has been a lot of speculation as to why the Bush Administration wants to go to war with Iraq and effect a "regime change." As has been discussed, it is clearly not because Iraq poses an imminent threat to the United States or its allies. Some critics have proposed a variety of other reasons for the war.

Was it because of the midterm 2002 Congressional elections? Generally, people do not change governments when facing war. While there may be some merit to that argument with regard to timing, U.S. aggression toward Iraq is about something much deeper than just affecting the result of the elections. Nor does the argument that war is a means of diverting attention from a failing economy adequately explain the incredible push for a war that carries substantial risks both at home and abroad. Again, this may be a partial answer to the question of "why now?" but it does not address the underlying rationale for going to war.

Equally unconvincing are explanations that going to war is a diversion from the U.S. failure to capture or kill Osama bin Laden and destroy Al Qaeda, or that Bush is completing the unfinished work of his father. While all of these proffered justifications hold some interest, none of them addresses the deeper nature of the current push for war: they do not address how the current policy results from the emergent U.S. role as *the* dominating superpower in a unipolar world where no single enemy can militarily challenge it.

The explanations lie elsewhere. After World Wars I and II, the victors redrew the map of the world. They did so to insure their worldwide dominance, their control over natural resources, and for other strategic reasons as well. For example, after World War I, the British took over substantial portions of the Ottoman Empire. Britain consolidated three separate provinces into the country of Iraq, and placed in power a King from the Hashemite royal family who was to become essentially a British puppet monarch. After World War II, the Russians and the United States redrew the map of Europe to suit their interests.

A similar phenomenon is occurring today after the end of the cold war. The map of the world is being redrawn primarily to fit the interests of the United States, the "victor" of the cold war. Germany is no longer divided, and the Soviet Union has fragmented into many countries. With the war in Afghanistan, the United States is now in a position to dominate Central Asia, including the former Soviet Republics of Kazakhstan, Uzbekistan, and Turkmenistan, where it is stationing troops and building military bases. The United States now has the ability to build and run an oil pipeline through Afghanistan and thereby control one of the world's larger sources of oil.

The U.S. effort to effect a "regime change" in Iraq must be seen in this light. The Bush Administration seeks to redraw the map of the Middle East in the way that best suits its own interests, and there is no opposing force capable of preventing it from doing so.

There are a number of reasons the United States wants to dominate Iraq, but primary among them is oil. The history of American involvement with Iraq bears this out. Until the Iraqi revolution of 1958, Iraq's oil was split five ways: 23.75 percent each went to Britain, France, Holland, and the

United States, and 5 percent went to the oil baron who negotiated the agreement that divided the spoils in the aftermath of World War I.[21] After the revolution, the United States employed many different strategies designed to weaken Iraq, including providing massive military support to the Kurdish groups fighting Baghdad.

After Saudi Arabia, Iraq has the largest proven oil reserves in the world. Controlling Iraq will give the United States access to this oil. It will also permit the United States to lessen the influence of OPEC and Saudi Arabia, and to facilitate America's near complete domination of the Middle East. Other countries, even allies such as France and Russia, will need to negotiate with the United States to get the oil they need—whether it is from Central Asia or the Middle East. China will also need to strike a deal with the United States for oil. The United States then would not only have the strongest military force in the world, but it would also control one of the world's most important resources.

There is also a deeper significance to an American war on Iraq, the call for a pre-emptive strike, and the willingness of the United States to go it alone militarily without the imprimatur of international institutions such as the United Nations. Two days after the passage of Security Council Resolution 1441—the new inspection resolution—the United States started insisting that it did not need U.N. permission to attack and that the resolution alone constituted a green light for war if Iraq did not fully comply. Although earlier administrations have expressed some willingness to ignore international institutions and international law, the Bush Administration is open and notorious about its views on this issue and its willingness to act unilaterally.

The planned war on Iraq must be understood within this context. More than a decade ago, when Dick Cheney and Paul Wolfowitz worked in the Pentagon for Bush I, they were already setting forth a plan for a post-Soviet world that focused on pre-emptive strikes and imposing U.S. will on the rest of the world through military might. Their plan was set forth in a series of government policy papers entitled "Defense Planning Guidance." These documents, which date from the early 1990s, have been reconstituted by the current Administration.[22]

President Bush, in various speeches, has reiterated the policy set forth in these documents. For example, in his June 2002 speech to the graduating class at West Point, Bush elaborated upon the idea first articulated in his State of the Union address, in which he warned the "axis of evil" nations that the United States would not wait "while dangers gather," and articulated a doctrine of pre-emptive strikes. This radical new approach proclaims that the United States may use military force against any state it perceives to be hostile; any state which seeks to acquire biological, chemical, or nuclear weapons; or any one that "aids" terrorism. What Bush has termed a new doctrine[23] is, as one senior U.S. military official put it, "the first time you've had a president say, 'We'll strike first.' It's a major change to publicly say that…"[24]

A recent article in *Harpers* magazine describes Bush's new doctrine in chilling terms:

> The Plan is for the United States to rule the world. The overt theme is unilateralism, but it is ultimately a story of domination. It calls for the United States to maintain its overwhelming military superiority and prevent new rivals from rising up to challenge it on the international stage. It calls for the dominion over friends and enemies alike. It says not that the United States must be more powerful, or most powerful, but that it must be absolutely powerful.[25]

The planned war and conquest of Iraq is also illustrative of the plans that the current U.S. government has for the rest of the world. The U.S. policy of pre-emptive strikes and military domination may well cause other countries to develop weapons of mass destruction; in turn, the world becomes increasingly insecure for all of us.

II. WHAT ABOUT THE LAW? IS IT LEGAL FOR THE UNITED STATES TO GO TO WAR WITH IRAQ?

We look to three bodies of law to determine whether the planned war against Iraq is legal: U.S. domestic law, international treaty law, and fundamental norms of customary international law. In this section, we will examine the legal obligations of the United States and the Bush Administration, as well as how those obligations relate to the planned war against Iraq.

The Law of the United States: the Necessity for Congressional Authorization

The U.S. Constitution gives Congress the power to decide when to go to war against another nation. In Article 1, Section 8, the U.S. Constitution gives Congress the power, "[t]o declare war, grant letters of marque and reprisal, and make rules concerning captures on land and water."[26] As a general matter, if Congress properly authorizes the President to employ military force or go to war, it is sufficient to satisfy Constitutional requirements. In other words, the President is required to obtain the consent of Congress before beginning a war. The rationale for granting this power to Congress and not the President alone was the framers' fear of lodging such an important decision in one person. They understood the dangers of war and wanted to make it difficult to initiate.

In the current situation with Iraq, the President did go to Congress to request authorization, and Congress gave its approval. In the preamble of the resulting resolution, the U.S. relationship with Iraq since the Persian Gulf War is reviewed, the actions Congress has taken regarding Iraq are detailed, and the resolution mentions everything from Iraq's alleged attempt to kill President Bush's father to the September 11 terrorist attacks.[27] This text is a model of exaggerated propaganda against Iraq, particularly with regard to any supposed threat to the United States from Iraq. The resolution "supports" the President's efforts to work with the United Nations Security Council to enforce U.N. Security Council resolutions and ensure that Iraq complies.[28] However, this section only indicates Congressional support for working with the United Nations; there is no requirement to get U.N. approval to go to war.

Section 3 of the resolution is the critical one. It gives the President the authority to go to war: "The President is authorized to use the Armed Forces of the United States as he determines to be necessary and appropriate in order to (1) defend the national security of the United States against the continuing threat posed by Iraq; and (2) enforce all relevant United Nations Security Council resolutions regarding Iraq."[29] The resolution further states that the President will determine when the United States can no longer rely on diplomatic means to settle the Iraq question. This gives the President the unique authority to determine when Iraq is a sufficient threat to warrant an attack, and to decide by himself when he believes it is necessary to enforce U.N. resolutions. He is not required to get Security Council approval for his actions, nor to consult with the Congress about the situation. He is only required to report every 60 days about his activities.[30]

The President has been given the authorization required by the U.S. Constitution. However, this Congressional authorization of force, as is explained below, is contrary to the terms of the U.N. Charter. Despite this, such a resolution is not illegal under U.S. domestic law. Laws passed by Congress and signed by the President override the terms of any treaty to the contrary. Although that is remarkable, it is true. However, while it may be that Congress can override the terms in treaties, it cannot override certain unwritten fundamental rules of customary international law (called jus cogens norms) that are binding on Congress and the President. For example, if Congress passed a law authorizing torture, it might well override treaty obligations but it will still run afoul of this unwritten fundamental international law. The prohibition against aggressive war, like that against torture, is such a fundamental international law. Congress does not have the authority to authorize an openly aggressive war.

The Law of the U.N. Charter: the Necessity for U.N. Security Council Authorization

The U.N. Charter, a treaty of the United States ratified by almost every country in the world, prohibits the use of force by one country against another except in two situations. The first is in the case of self-defense; the second is with U.N. Security Council approval. This major change in international law was implemented in the wake of World War II and essentially outlawed war except in the narrowest of circumstances. While during the 40-year cold war both the Soviet Union and the United States violated the Charter's prohibition on the use of force in defense of perceived national interests, both superpowers at least gave lip service to the Charter's prohibition of the use of force except in self-defense. Although, on November 8, 2002, the Security Council approved a resolution regarding an enhanced inspection regime for Iraq, that resolution does not authorize the use of force.

Self-Defense

Article 51 of the Charter sets forth the exception for self-defense.[31] A nation can employ self-defense only "if an armed attack occurs,"[32] or, as a number of authorities have argued, in response to an imminent attack—conditions which nobody asserts exist in the Iraq situation. None of the reasons given by the Bush Administration or Congress for attacking Iraq, including destruction of claimed weapons of mass destruction or overthrowing Saddam Hussein, constitute self-defense under the U.N. Charter.[33] Nor does the language of the authorization given by Congress meet the test for self-defense: employment of force to "defend the national security of the United States against the continuing threat posed by Iraq," is not a description of an armed or imminent attack on the United States.

Bush Administration's New Doctrine of Pre-emptive Strikes

In the new Bush doctrine described in the section above, President Bush proclaims that the United States can use military force against any state that the Administration perceives to be hostile. This new U.S. position, obviously aimed at justifying an attack on Iraq, is a public renunciation of the U.N. Charter's limitation on the use of force.

Pre-emptive strikes are different from an earlier doctrine that was labeled "anticipatory self-defense" under which the United States and some other countries argued that they had the right under the U.N. Charter to attack a country that was planning an armed attack. This latter doctrine at least gave lip service to the restrictions on the use of force embodied in the Charter—that force could only be used in self-defense or as authorized by the Security Council under Article 42. The new doctrine of pre-emptive strikes moves beyond the restrictions of the Charter by stating that force will be used even if there is no immediate threat. It may well take the world back to a period prior to World War I and the U.N. Charter, when the employment of force had no legal restraints; countries could use military violence when and where they wanted.

The Bush Administration and now the Congress have abandoned the U.N. Charter's core legal restraints in favor of a system in which the United States unilaterally decides matters of war and peace, and which regimes warrant replacement by force. By at least rhetorically supporting the heart of the U.N. system over the past 54 years, the United States has supported its continuance. The doctrine of pre-emptive strikes wounds the U.N. system irrevocably. The consequences of this new doctrine are frightening and will result in the exercise of unabashed imperial power. This path will lead to more terror against the peoples of the world and the people of the United States. War with Iraq without U.N. authorization will represent a tragic day in our nation's history, and could prove to be disastrous to world peace and security.

U.N. Authorization

The other justification of military action against a nation is U.N. approval and authorization under Chapter VII of the U.N. Charter, specifically Articles 42 and 43. Obtaining authority for war from the U.N. Security Council is not merely a political nicety; it is a legal requirement. Short of receiving explicit authority from the United Nations, the use of force by the United States against Iraq, even with the recent Congressional approval, would be blatantly illegal under international law. No resolution, including the U.N. resolution passed on November 8, 2002, authorizes the use of force.

As mentioned above, the Congressional authorization to "enforce all relevant United Nations resolutions regarding Iraq," is not the U.N. approval required for unilateral action, nor do Iraqi violations of past U.N. resolutions give the United States the legal authority to attack. The Security Council, not individual countries, determines whether Iraq has breached its agreements and what is to be done about those breaches. The authority of the Security Council was established and agreed to by the United States and every other U.N. member upon signing and ratifying the U.N. Charter. This arrangement prioritizes multilateral, international responses to world events over unilateral reactions.

Many U.N. Resolutions, 1990–2001: None Authorize Force Today

Since the United States cannot unilaterally enforce U.N. resolutions, the Security Council must explicitly agree to any proposed military action in order for it to be legal. That has not happened yet. Nor do any of the past resolutions condone military action against Iraq now. In November of 1990, the Security Council approved Resolution 678, authorizing the United States and other states to use force to oust Iraq from Kuwait. Resolution 678 also contained other language, common in U.N. resolutions, permitting states to "restore international peace and security in the area."[34]

Over the years, the United States has used that language to authorize a variety of actions. However, the words were never intended to create a state of permanent war in an entire region. The language is vague; "the region" could be Iraq, Iraq/Kuwait, or the entire Middle East, and "restore international peace" has multiple connotations.[35] The original intent and purpose of the resolution was achieved many years ago: ousting Iraq from Kuwait. It cannot be used to go beyond its original purpose.

After the war ended, the Security Council in April 1991 passed Resolution 687 recognizing the cease-fire, directing Iraq to surrender all weapons of mass destruction, and creating an inspections regime, UNSCOM, to effect compliance. The current Bush Administration is now trying to use the *prior* resolution, 678, as a justification for its planned use of force. Yet, Resolution 678 clearly gives *no* authority to any country to enforce the subsequent resolution, 687. That decision would need to be made by the Security Council.

In March of 1998, the Security Council passed Resolution 1154. That resolution threatened "severest consequences" for Iraq if any future violations of the inspection regime occurred. The Council retained the authority to ensure implementation, and it was for the Council, not individual countries, to decide whether to make good on that threat. The Council never did so. The majority of states involved in creating Resolution 1154 stated that additional Security Council authorization would be necessary before force could be used for alleged violations of the inspection regime.[36]

In summary, despite the history of U.N. resolutions about Iraq, no authority exists on which the United States could legally base a military attack.

The Current Resolution: U.N. Resolution 1441: Still No Authorization

On November 8, 2002, after almost eight weeks of negotiation and tremendous pressure by the United States, the United Nations unanimously adopted Resolution 1441 establishing a new timetable and a new regime of inspections for Iraq. What it did not do is authorize any country to use force against Iraq. The United States still must, as a matter of law, go back to the U.N. Security Council for authority to use force. Its claim that it need not do so is not law; it is an assertion of sheer power.

A number of countries, particularly France and Russia, wanted a two-resolution answer to the Iraq issue. The first resolution would set out the terms of the inspection, but not authorize war. A second meeting of the Security Council would then be required to determine whether Iraq had breached the first resolution and the consequences for such a breach. The United States wanted a one-stage resolution. It wanted the resolution to require both new inspections as well as give authority for war, without any need to return to the Security Council. The resolution that was eventually passed might be called a one and one-half stage resolution.

The United States got much of what it wanted, but it did not get the clear authority to go to war with Iraq if there was a failure in the inspection regime. The opposing countries got some of what they wanted; the inspectors are to report back to the Security Council, which will then consider the situation. From a legal perspective, a war without a second U.N. resolution authorizing it will be an illegal war.

However, this is not a legal interpretation accepted by the United States. The United States has argued that it does not need any authority from the United Nations to go to war against Iraq, and it also claims that Resolution 1441 gives it that authority. The United States was successful in getting language into the resolution from which it claims it will have the authority to attack Iraq for even the most minor inspection disputes.

First, the United States insisted, and the Council did decide, that Iraq "was and remains" in "material breach," of prior resolutions including Resolution 687, the cease-fire resolution.[37] The United States will argue that the cease-fire under Resolution 687 is no longer in effect and therefore the legal status reverts to Resolution 678, the use of force resolution. Of course, as has been pointed out, Resolution 678 was about ousting Iraq from Kuwait and not about using force to enforce the inspections regime.

Second, Resolution 1441 also decides that any future "false statements or omissions...and failure by Iraq at any time to comply with, and cooperate fully in the implementation of, this resolution shall constitute a further material breach."[38] The decision to use this language to define Iraq's behavior is remarkable. It means that any dispute or the most minor problem with the inspections is defined as a "material breach" of the resolution. A traffic jam on a highway to a site to be inspected could be deemed interference with inspectors and a material breach.

However, even if it deemed that any minor infraction constitutes a material breach, it is still up to the Security Council to decide the consequences for such a breach. The United States did get some clever language that it is sure to use as an additional legal argument as to why it can bypass the Council and decide unilaterally to use force. Paragraph 13 states that the Council has "repeatedly warned Iraq that it will face serious consequences as a result of its continued violations of its obligations." The United States is sure to argue that "serious consequences" means that it can employ military force for violations of the inspection regime. However, standard diplomatic language used in U.N. resolutions to authorize force is "all necessary means." The Security Council used that phrase in its 1990 resolution authorizing the United States to oust Iraq from Kuwait. There is a strong argument that "serious consequences" does not include the use of violence.

This compromised language appears to have satisfied both sides. By parsing the language of the resolution, the Bush Administration believes it can justify attacking Iraq. Although the United States did agree to come back to the Security Council for discussion, it does not believe that it *needs* to do so in order to initiate a war.[39] After all, the resolution does not require a subsequent resolution to authorize military action.[40] Of course, it should not need to. Affirmative authority from the Council is required for war; absence of authority is not authorization for war. France, Russia, and China all released statements that Resolution 1441 excludes "automaticity" in the use of force."[41] They go on to emphasize that only the Security Council has the ability to respond to a misstep by Iraq.

How This Resolution Came About: Oil, Coercion, and Bribery

The Security Council legal process is political, much like that of our own Congress. In the recent unanimous vote regarding Resolution 1441, intense desire for increased access to cheap oil more than likely played a major part in the U.S. ability to finally obtain favorable votes from

France, Russia, and possibly China. Those countries may have strongly preferred relying on the inspection regime and a U.N. resolution that clearly prohibited force without a second Security Council resolution. But, once the United States expressed that it wanted a regime change—and would acquire it by force if necessary—France, Russia, and China were put in a serious bind. Russia has some seven billion dollars invested in Iraq, and numerous oil deals awaiting the day for the embargo to be lifted. France, likewise, has such oil deals, and is already obtaining a significant amount of oil from Iraq.

Numerous articles have already appeared stating that following a U.S. occupation of Iraq, American oil companies will get first crack at Iraqi oil.[42] Numerous articles have also documented that Russia and France are concerned that their oil contracts will not be honored if and when the United States occupies Iraq. Those contracts will *not* be honored if France and Russia try to obstruct the path of the United States.[43] So, in the end, those countries can protest a bit, but they cannot hold out. Oil, and economic and military power will win the day for the United States.

Nor is the United States beyond employing coercion and bribery to get its way in the Security Council. This not only taints the process that was set up by the U.N. Charter to peacefully resolve conflicts, it illegitimates its decisions. The United States used coercive measures to secure support for the 1991 war with Iraq, and this was surely not lost on the members of the Council. They surely all recalled the vote on the 1990 Iraq resolution that authorized the use of force. When Yemen voted against it, the U.S. envoy turned to the Yemeni ambassador and said that it was "the most expensive 'no' vote you would ever cast." The United States then cut off its entire 70 million dollar aid program to Yemen.

The coercion was so blatant in 1990 that U.S. Representative Henry Gonzalez submitted an impeachment resolution and brief[44] that detailed the bribes and threats. He noted U.S. coercion against the Soviet Union, Zaire, Egypt, Syria, Saudi Arabia, and Yemen. In addition, the United States, which owes more money to the United Nations than any other nation, paid off $187 million of its debt immediately after the vote authorizing the use of force.

What kind of free choice is there for the Security Council after Bush has repeatedly referred to the United Nations as weak and ineffectual, and has indicated that with or without approval the United States will act according to its own wishes? The Security Council is given very little choice in that situation—it is then essentially forced to conform to the will of the only super-power in the world. How much better, though, would it be if the countries of the Council could make a choice based upon law and what is right?

Ultimately, the United Nations may or may not provide a resolution authorizing military force against Iraq. If it invades Iraq without the authorization of a resolution, the United States will be committing a major violation of the U.N. Charter. If a resolution is forthcoming, but the United States continues with its coercive tactics and its sheer use of power, any authority granted will be compromised.

A Security Council Vote To Authorize War Against Iraq May Violate Fundamental Norms of International Law

Even if the United States obtained Security Council support for a unilateral attack, the attack itself could violate what the legal profession calls jus cogens norms. Jus cogens norms, as stated previously, are the most basic fundamental international laws, such as the rejection of genocide or slavery, and are accepted throughout the world. Jus cogens means "compelling law" and in practice is an international legal standard that no country can opt out of or avoid. Aggressive war is a violation of a jus cogens norm.[45]

A crime against peace, or aggressive war, is a fundamental tenet of international law for several reasons. This is one of the crimes the Nazis were tried for at Nuremburg. Although some people argued this law had not been clarified before World War II, people felt and still feel today that the Nazis' actions were a clear violation of international law. They certainly would be today.

In addition, crimes against peace are banned in the U.N. Charter, a treaty that is almost universally ratified, so the world as a whole maintains that aggressive war is against the law. Neither the United States nor the United Nations can act contrary to these fundamental tenets of international law.[46] They bind all countries and the United Nations as well.

III. ALTERNATIVES TO THE USE OF FORCE

If Saddam Hussein's Iraq is a threat to our well-being in the future, that does not mean we need to jeopardize the lives of Iraqis and Americans in order to defuse that threat. Other options exist, including: weapons inspections and containment, using international law fora, a Weapons-of-Mass-Destruction–Free Zone throughout the Middle East, universal disarmament, and diplomacy.

Weapons Inspections

The first and most obvious option as an alternative to the use of violence is for the United States to put its full support behind the weapons inspections process.

In the past, weapons inspections have been effective. Even despite Iraq's uncooperative stance regarding the inspections, in UNSCOM's last inspections report in 1999, Richard Butler stated, "As has been reported to the Council, over the years, and as has been widely recognized, notwithstanding the very considerable obstacles placed by Iraq in the way of the Commission's work, a great deal has been achieved in: verifying Iraq's frequently revised declarations; accounting for its proscribed weapons capabilities; and in destroying, removing or rendering harmless substantial portions of that capability."[47] Not only were the inspections successful, but ultimately they were more effective than bombing in approaching the goal of disarming Iraq.

Security Council Resolution 1441 calls for Iraq to concede even more than it has in past resolutions, including those passed at the end of hostilities in the Gulf War. Resolution 1441 imposes many far-reaching requirements upon Iraq. For example, the resolution required a very specific report from Iraq on all of its weapons by December 8, 2002, only thirty days after the resolution date—a substantial task. The resolution also gives "immediate, unimpeded, unrestricted, and private access" for U.N. weapons inspectors: for instance, inspectors can transport Iraqis and their families outside of Iraq for interviews without the presence of representatives from the Iraqi government.

Iraq acceded to all of these requirements when it accepted the terms of Resolution 1441. Weapons inspections can and will provide an excellent means to establish the status of Iraq's weapons of mass destruction programs while also avoiding the horrors of war. Yet the Bush Administration waits expectantly for the first misstep—rhetorically supporting the inspection process, but indicating its readiness to attack should the least requirement go unfulfilled. Thus, the disingenuous nature of Resolution 1441 is that it not only indicates a false intention to end the conflict peaceably, but is in fact designed to be so complicated and invasive that it is intended to fail.

Building Respect for International Law

If Iraq is in violation of the international law prohibiting the buildup of weapons of mass destruction, there are avenues to prosecute these violations rather than war. Past U.S. conduct suggests that a U.S. attack will create an enormous number of civilian casualties, and many violations of the laws of war prohibiting civilian targeting and disproportionate use of force. A war against Iraq prosecutes the entire country rather than the leaders who have actually perpetrated crimes.

Its conflict with Iraq provides the United States

with a powerful opportunity to demonstrate a commitment to building respect for the rule of law. Building the rule of law is a key component to making the world safer, rather than contributing to lawlessness and the rule of sheer military power.

In the past, the United States has shown that it is willing to turn to international legal institutions to provide justice for those who have suffered at the hands of repressive regimes. The United States was a key participant in the trials of Nazi war criminals in Nuremberg, Germany, and Japanese war criminals in Tokyo, Japan, after World War II, and it took an active role in creating the ad hoc International Criminal Tribunal for the Former Yugoslavia to try individuals suspected of genocide, war crimes, and crimes against humanity in Bosnia, Herzegovina in the early-mid 1990s. It supported the International Criminal Tribunal for Rwanda for individuals suspected of participation in the 1994 genocide in that country. These courts have the powers to investigate, extradite, and issue warrants of arrest. If the United States is convinced that Saddam Hussein and members of the Iraqi government are international outlaws, it can go to the Security Council and ask for the power to prosecute them. While some will claim that these tribunals are "inherently political," basing them on the principles of international law provides sound reasons for choosing this option.

There are also options in U.S. courts, which are currently in use. Iraq is one of the countries that can be sued as part of an exception to the Foreign Sovereign Immunities Act. Individuals can be sued under the Alien Tort Claims Act,[48] part of U.S. law since 1789, and the recently enacted Torture Victim Protection Act.[49] There are no fewer than three pending class-action lawsuits charging violations of these statutes for the victims of the 9/11 attacks.[50] As discussed above, if Iraq is in violation of international law, its government can be sued for its violations.

There is also the opportunity to turn to the emerging International Criminal Court. Unfortunately, the Bush Administration has been one of the governments most opposed to establishing an international body to charge international outlaws with responsibility for egregious international law violations. However, it is international institutions such as these that provide the hope for a consistent rule of law for all.

Universal Disarmament[51]

True protection from nuclear, biological, and chemical weapons attacks would happen if all countries universally disarmed. The United States has not acted to further this, and in fact has acted in contradiction to the Non-Proliferation Treaty, and others. The world will only be safe from nuclear, biological, and chemical weapons when they no longer exist; universal disarmament is the safest—and best—path for all human beings.

Weapons-of-Mass-Destruction–Free Zone[52]

Even if universal disarmament is not immediately possible, regional disarmament could lead to increased safety. In Security Council Resolution 687, paragraph 14, the Council set the goal of the creation of a Weapons-of-Mass-Destruction–Free Zone throughout the region of the Middle East. The imbalance of weaponry in the Middle East has made it a very dangerous area and has encouraged the development of further weapons technology throughout the region

The fact that Israel has such large and advanced weapons reserves[53] provides a threat to all Middle Eastern countries. As Stephen Shalom and Michael Albert state, "The acquisition of WMD by one state generally encourages, rather than discourages, their acquisition by others."[54] As long as some countries in the Middle East have weapons of mass destruction, other countries will be trying to acquire them. Furthering the goal of weapons-free zones is an alternative to military action that would be more likely to lead to the increased security and well-being of people throughout the world.

If U.S. security is truly felt to be at risk, at the very least, the Bush Administration should meet with Iraqi officials[55] and actually discuss what can be done to to decrease the threat. The vast majority of conflicts over arms buildups are dealt with through negotiations, and this case should be no exception.

North Korea, another country excoriated by the Bush Administration, recently announced that it has nuclear weapons. The reaction from the Bush Administration was measured and diplomatic.[56] The Administration plans to begin talks with North Korea about disarmament, but first met with its allies in the region who have an interest in the outcome of this situation. The response of the U.S. government in this case was multilateral, fair, and diplomatic. Before war— and all of the calamities that come with it—the United States should first exhaust all venues of diplomacy.

IV. CONSEQUENCES OF WAR

Despite heavy criticism and cautionary advice from domestic and international voices, the Bush Administration is continuing its plans for an illegal war against Iraq. It is no secret that the United States is already working on a plan of attack that will guarantee the ouster of Iraq's current government, and its replacement, at least for the fore-seeable future, by a U.S. occupation government. Lieutenant General Thomas McInerney, former assistant vice chief of staff of the U.S. Air Force, calls for blitz warfare to be used in Iraq. He elaborates, "Blitz warfare is an intensive 24-hour, seven-days-a-week precision air-centric campaign supported by fast moving ground forces composed of a mixture of heavy, light, airborne, amphibious, special, covert operations that all use effects-based base operations for their target set and correlate their timing of forces for a devastating violent impact...."[57]

It is clear that the Bush Administration views a "devastating violent impact" in Iraq as a victory for the United States; it is developing a plan for blitz warfare by the Central Command in Tampa, Florida.[58] In its haste for war, the Bush Administration is purposely ignoring the severe ramifications that an invasion of Iraq by the United States will produce.

Human Casualties

Since the end of the Gulf War, it is estimated that 1.27 million innocent Iraqi civilians have been killed as a result of the economic sanctions that are still in effect.[59] The sanctions visited upon Iraq have led to severe cases of malnutrition and shortages of medicines resulting in a 100 percent increase of the infant mortality rate.[60] Iraq has been losing from 5,000 to 6,000 children every month.[61] U.S. forces destroyed much of the electrical and sanitation infrastructure in the last war and the sanctions have prevented Iraq from making the necessary repairs. Bombings during the Gulf War were found to violate international law prohibitions against attacking civilian targets and the use of proportionate force.[62] If the United States goes ahead with the massive air and ground assault it is intending to unleash on Iraq, it could easily demolish the remaining infrastructure so necessary to human health, opening the door to the loss of more innocent lives.

Most startling, however, is the utter refusal of those calling for a war against Iraq to address any of the human and political consequences of a U.S. war. No one can say for sure what the effects on the Iraqi people will be from an assault of massive violence. It is very difficult to estimate the number of civilian casualties there will be, and the degree of damage to the country's infrastructure. Experts estimate (calculated from the prior Gulf War and other comparable conflicts) that "total possible deaths on all sides during a conventional conflict and the following three months [could] range from 48,000 to over 260,000."[63]

Due to the lack of support from opposition groups in Iraq and little support from its allies, the

United States is going to have to deploy from 200,000 to 300,000 American troops in order to achieve a successful invasion and occupation of Iraq. Kurdish forces from the north of Iraq and Shiite groups from the south have been fighting against Saddam Hussein's oppressive regime for years. They also possess deep mistrust of the U.S. government as they have been repeatedly betrayed by Washington. They are far outnumbered by groups within Iraq who would like to see the survival of Saddam Hussein's regime. These groups include the Ba'ath party and its supporters, security and intelligence personnel, and core elements of the armed forces and their extended families.[64] It is likely that this conflict is going to turn bloody as Saddam Hussein and his supporters fight to maintain power. The defense of Iraq, particularly of Baghdad, is going to cause American casualties in the thousands. Once again, communities of color will be commanded to bear the brunt of the war.[65]

Risk of a Wider War in the Middle East

A U.S. war on Iraq poses serious risks to the already highly volatile Middle East. It is reasonably feared that the United States might very well drive Iraq into attacking its regional neighbors, including Israel. Prime Minister Ariel Sharon of Israel has made it clear that this time Israel will respond to any Iraqi threat—unlike in 1991 when Israel was hit by 39 Iraqi scud missiles and restrained itself from retaliating. Prime Minister Sharon believes this was interpreted as weakness by Israel's enemies.[66] Both Palestinians and Israelis anticipate negative impacts on Palestinians living under occupation, including mass expulsions from their homes.[67]

Making the United States and the World Less Safe

There is no doubt that a war against Iraq by the United States will substantially increase anti-American sentiment within fundamentalist Islamic groups in the region and elsewhere. Terrorism in the United States and the rest of the world will increase; it already has because of U.S. saber rattling. In October and December of 2002, as war fever intensified, terrorism against U.S. and Western targets substantially increased. The bombing in Bali killed hundreds; a U.S. soldier was killed in Kuwait; a U.S. diplomat was murdered in Jordan; a French tanker was bombed off the coast of Yemen, and a car bomb killed 16 in Mombasa, Kenya, minutes after two missiles narrowly missed an Israeli-chartered plane leaving Mombasa's airport. The leaders of Al Qaeda, both bin Laden and Ayman al-Zawahiri, have threatened more attacks on "America and its allies" for the threatened attack on Iraq.[68]

Some have argued that these terrorist attacks would occur in any case, but even U.S. officials

RATNER, GREEN, OLSHANSKY

acknowledge that the threats against Iraq may well be a cause of renewed terrorism. An October 2002 *Wall Street Journal* article states that "[o]ne reason for renewed activity, a U.S. counter-terrorism official said, may be the Bush Administration's moves toward possible military conflict with Iraq."[69]

And with a full-scale war, there is no doubt that the United States must be ready for a major increase in terrorism. The government is planning to activate 265,000 National Guard and Reserve troops for the war. The majority will not be used for the offensive against Iraq, but for defending vulnerable locations in the United States, including power plants, airports, hospitals, transportation facilities, and symbolic landmarks.[70] This is a clear acknowledgment that the Bush Administration recognizes that a pre-emptive war on Iraq intensifies the likelihood of terrorism, retaliation, and counterattacks against the United States and its allies.

U.S. Economy

Much media attention has been given to Iraq's rich oil resources during the Bush Administration's campaign for a war against Iraq. By having the world's second largest oil reserve, estimated at 112 billion barrels, and additional undiscovered oil reserves, Iraq plays a key role in the global energy market.[71] The dialogue in the mainstream media has been biased in focusing mainly on the profits to be made post-war, and not on the negative effects the war with Iraq will produce on the domestic economy of the United States.

The United States' desire to go to war with Iraq has produced negative outcomes for U.S. consumers who are already suffering from a weakened economy that is barely emerging from last year's recession. The price for oil is increasing as the attack on Iraq becomes more imminent and unavoidable. Following the 1990–1991 Gulf War, oil prices not only doubled but also stayed high for months after, and a repeat of the conflict is likely to cause the same effect.[72]

The lack of support that the United States is receiving from its allies in Europe and in the Middle East will be very costly for the U.S economy. During the Gulf War, 80 percent of the war's cost was covered by U.S. allies. Congressional budget experts estimate that fighting a full-scale war could cost the United States close to nine billion dollars a month.[73]

International Influence

As the world's sole superpower, the United States exerts major influence on other countries. In addition to the ramifications described above, an important example of this influence took place after the September 11 terrorist attacks on the

United States. The anti-terrorist measures that were taken by President Bush and Attorney General John Ashcroft have resulted in a serious erosion of civil liberties and human rights within the United States. For example, new laws were introduced criminalizing political dissent, allowing arbitrary and indefinite detention of non-citizens and monitoring of attorney-client communications, and setting up special military commissions that try suspected terrorists.[74] Many countries around the globe are attempting to take advantage of the United States' version of the war on terrorism by prosecuting their own political opponents, separatists, and religious groups. Some of the countries that have followed the United States' footsteps in curtailing and violating civil liberties and human rights are Australia, Belarus, China, Egypt, India, Israel, Jordan, Kyrgyzstan, Macedonia, Malaysia, Russia, Syria, Uzbekistan, and Zimbabwe.[75]

By waging an illegal pre-emptive strike on Iraq, the United States is sending a message that obstructs the United Nations system, international cooperation, and alternative ways to conflict resolution. There is a serious risk that other countries will follow this negative precedent of the United States by waging illegal pre-emptive strikes on their elected enemies.[76]

In Conclusion

The United States should reconsider its campaign for this illegal and aggressive war on Iraq, as it bears costly ramifications. Instead of rushing to violence, the United States should carefully explore alternative ways of resolving this conflict.

VI. INFORMATION AND ACTION

Things We Can DO

➤ Attend rallies for peace in your area. Better yet, organize rallies in your area. Get in touch with national organizations, like International A.N.S.W.E.R. (www.internationalanswer.org), End the War, or Not in Our Name, to get started.

➤ Organize and attend teach-ins in your community—help other people learn about the issues.

➤ Talk to your friends and family about the actions of the United States government and what is happening in Iraq.

➤ Write letters to your member of Congress, as well as the President and his staff, about your position on the war on Iraq. Thoughtful, unique letters go a long way with your representatives. Be aware of how your representatives stand on this issue. See www.vote.com for more information.

➤ Wear a pin or fly a flag demonstrating your support for a peaceful international response to Iraq. Be willing and able to discuss your position when someone asks about it.

➤ Write letters to the editor and ask to meet with editorial boards. Respond to the articles you see in your local press.

➤ Make financial contributions to groups whose ideas you support or organize events to raise money for those groups.

➤ Meet with your legislators in groups to explain your position. See the Global Exchange website, www.globalexchange.org, for more information on how to do this effectively.

➤ Stay informed and inform others. Your knowledge counteracts ignorance and apathy.

➤ Use your own special talents to help the cause: if you have legal training, help political detainees; if you knit, send hats for children to Iraq; if you act, do street theatre to educate other people in your community.

➤ Lobby U.N. Security Council members and ask them to prioritize the rule of law.

Things you can READ for more information

Anthony Arnove, ed.; *Iraq Under Seige, The Deadly Impact of Sanctions and War, Updated Edition* (South End Press: 2002).

Phyllis Bennis, *All the Facts About Iraq*, ALTER-NET (Aug. 15, 2002), *at* www.alternet.org/story.html?StoryID=13859.

Phyllis Bennis, *The Bush Proposal to the United Nations*, Institute for Policy Studies, *at* http://www.tni.org/fellow/bennis.html (Sept. 29, 2002).

Jay Bookman, "The President's Real Goal in Iraq," *The Atlanta Journal-Constitution*, Sept. 29, 2002.

Nancy Chang, *Silencing Political Dissent: How Post-September 11 Anti-Terrorism Measures Threaten Our Civil Liberties* (Seven Stories Press/ Open Media Series: 2002).

"Iraq," Energy Information Administration, *available at* http://www.eia.doe.gov/emeu/cabs/iraqfull.html (Dec. 1999).

Richard Falk, "A Dangerous Game," *The Nation*, Oct. 7, 2002.

Lewis H. Lapham, "The Road to Babylon: Searching for Targets in Iraq," *Harper's Magazine*, Oct. 1, 2002.

Jules Lobel & Michael Ratner, "Bypassing the Security Council: Ambiguous Authorizations to Use Force, Cease Fires, and the Iraqi Inspection Regime," *93 AM. J. INT'L L.* 124 (1999).

Dan Morgan & David B. Ottaway, "In Iraqi War Scenario, Oil Is Key Issue," *Washington Post*, Sept. 15, 2002.

Barbara Olshansky, Center for Constitutional Rights, *Secret Trials and Executions: Military Tribunals and the Threat to Democracy* (Seven Stories Press/ Open Media Series: 2002).

James A. Paul, *Iraq: The Struggle for Oil*, Global Policy Forum, *at*, http://www.globalpolicy.org/security/oil/2002/08jim.htm (Aug. 2002).

Miriam Pemberton, "FPIF Talking Points: The Economic Costs of a War with Iraq," *Foreign Policy In Focus* (Sept. 13, 2002), *at* http://www.fpif.org/cgaa/talkingpoings/0209ira qwarcost_body.html.

Rebuilding America's Defenses: Strategy, Forces and Resources For a New Century, Project for the New American Century, *at* http://www.newamericancentury.org/publica-tionsreports.htm (Sept. 2000) (laying out the military plan for a post-Soviet world that focuses on imposing U.S. will on the rest of the world through military might.)

Michael Ratner, *Making Us Less Free: War on Terrorism or War on Liberty?*, Center for Constitutional Rights, *at* http://www.human-rightsnow.org (May 1, 2002).

Michael Ratner, *War Crime Not Self-Defense: the Unlawful War Against Iraq*, Center for Constitutional Rights, *at* http://www.humanrightsnow.org (*last visited* Nov. 18, 2002).

Stephen R. Shalom & Michael Albert, *45 Questions and Answers Regarding Intervention in General, 9-11 and Afghanistan One Year Later, and Iraq on the Verge of War*, ZNet, *at* http://www.zmag.org/45qairaq.htm (Oct. 9, 2002).

The National Security Strategy of the United States of America, The White House, *at* http://www.whitehouse.gov/nsc/nss.pdf (Sept. 2002).

Stephen Zunes, "*Seven Reasons to Oppose a U.S. Invasion of Iraq*," FPIF Policy Report (Aug. 2002), *at* http://www.fpif.org/papers/iraq2_body.html.

Websites with More Information

AMERICAN FRIENDS SERVICE COMMITTEE
www.afsc.org
Provides detailed information regarding the proposed U.S. war against Iraq.

AMNESTY INTERNATIONAL
www.ai.org
Examines the human rights violations that result from the proposed war on Iraq by the United States.

CENTER FOR CONSTITUTIONAL RIGHTS
www.ccr-ny.org
General anti-war updates with focus on international human rights and civil liberties. CCR also provides legal assistance to U.S. detainees.

FOREIGN POLICY IN FOCUS
www.fpif.org
Analyzes U.S. foreign policy and relations using the proposed war against Iraq as an example.

HUMAN RIGHTS WATCH
www.hrw.org
Monitors and provides reports of human rights violations from around the globe.

INTERNATIONAL A.N.S.W.E.R.
www.internationalanswer.org
Contains a list of actions that the public can take in order to stop the war on Iraq.

MOVE ON
www.moveon.org
Advocates for the participation of the public in politics with a vision of changing U.S. domestic and foreign policy

NATIONAL NETWORK TO END THE WAR AGAINST IRAQ
www.endthewar.org
Organizes protests and non-violent civil disobedience.

NOT IN OUR NAME
www.notinourname.net
Proposes a Pledge of Resistance to use to structure protests and other anti-war actions and provides information about upcoming rallies.

PAX CHRISTI
www.paxchristiusa.org
Provides information about philosophical non-violence and spiritual forms of resistance in addition to actions citizens can take to protest the war.

UNITED NATIONS
www.un.org
The purposes of the United Nations, as set forth in the Charter, are to maintain international peace and security; to develop friendly relations among nations; to cooperate in solving international economic, social, cultural and humanitarian problems and in promoting respect for human rights and fundamental freedoms; and to be a center for harmonizing the actions of nations in attaining these ends.

UNITED NATIONS MONITORING, VERIFICATION AND INSPECTION COMMISSION
http://www.un.org/Depts/unmovic/
UNMOVIC is a replacement of the former UN Special Commission, and continues with the latter's mandate to disarm Iraq of its weapons of mass destruction (chemical, biological weapons and missiles with a range of more than 150 km), and

to operate a system of ongoing monitoring and verification to check Iraq's compliance with its obligations not to reacquire the same weapons prohibited to it by the Security Council.

NOTES

1. *See* Noam Chomsky & Michael Albert, *Interview With Noam Chomsky About U.S. Warplans*, ZNet, *at* http://www.zmag.org/content/showarticle.cfm?SectionID=15&ItemID=2422 (Aug. 29, 2002).
2. *See* Alan Simpson, MP & Dr. Glen Rangwala, *Labour Against the War's Counter-Dossier: The Dishonest Case for War on Iraq*, Labour Against the War, *at* http://www.labouragainstthewar.org.uk/ (September 27, 2002).
3. *Id.*
4. Senator Bob Graham, of the Senate Intelligence Committee, Senator Joseph Biden, and Senator Chuck Hagel, have all publicly questioned whether the Administration ever had the evidence officials have claimed. Pentagon officials have echoed this concern. Stephen R. Shalom & Michael Albert, *45 Questions and Answers Regarding Intervention in General, 9-11 and Afghanistan One Year Later, and Iraq on the Verge of War*, ZNet, at C3, *at* http://www.zmag.org/45qairaq.htm (Oct. 9, 2002).
5. *Id.* at C2; Anthony Cordesman, *The Military Balance in the Gulf*, Center for Strategic and International Studies, at 79, *at* http://www.iraqwatch.org/perspectives/csis-gulf-mil-2001.pdf (July 2001).
6. Shalom & Albert, *supra* note 4, at C2; *Id.* at 79.
7. *See* Chomsky & Albert, *supra* note 1.
8. *Id.*
9. Jules Lobel & Michael Ratner, "Bypassing the Security Council: Ambiguous Authorizations to Use Force, Cease-

Fires and the Iraqi Inspection Regime," 93 AM. J. INT'L L. 124, 132-33 (1999).

10. Simpson & Rangwala, *supra* note 2. *See also* http://www.iaea.or.at/worldatom/Programmes/Action-team for a description of IAEA activities.

11. *Id*.

12. The contention stated in the British dossier that Iraq is seeking uranium from Africa is wholly unsupported. No country and no year is specified, and South Africa, the only country that has the potential capacity for the enrichment of uranium to bomb quality, has stated that it has not supplied Iraq with such material. *See* "Detailed Analysis of October 7 Speech by Bush on Iraq," Institute for Public Accuracy, at 2, *at* www.accuracy.org/bush [*last visited* Nov. 18, 2002) [hereinafter "Detailed Analysis of October 7 Speech"].

13. President George W. Bush, Remarks by the President on Iraq, Address at the Cincinnati Museum Center (Oct. 7, 2002), *available at* http://www.whitehouse.gov/news/releases/2002/10/20021007-8.html.

14. Simpson & Rangwala, *supra* note 2.

15. Scott Ritter, "The Case for Iraq's Qualitative Disarmament," *Arms Control Today*, June 2000 (written by the former head of UNSCOM's Concealment Unit).

16. Anthony H. Cordesman, "Iraq's Past and Future Biological Weapons Capabilities," Center for Strategic and International Studies, at 13, *at* http://www.csis.org/mideast/reports/iraq_bios.pdf (Feb. 1998).

17. Simpson & Rangwala, *supra* note 2.

18. *Id*. (citing Charles Duefer, former U.S. Deputy Assistant Secretary of State, and deputy head of UNSCOM).

19. "Detailed Analysis of October 7 Speech," *supra* note 12, at 5 (quoting Chris Toensing, editor of *Middle East Report*).

20. Alison Mitchell & Carl Hulse, "C.I.A. Sees Terror After Iraq Action," *New York Times*, Oct. 9, 2002, at A1.

21. *See* Richard Becker, "The U.S. & Iraq: A History," International Action Center, *at* http://www.iacenter.org/iraq_history.htm (Oct. 19, 2002).

22. David Armstrong, "Dick Cheney's Song of America," *Harper's Magazine,* Sept. 2002; "Rebuilding America's Defenses: Strategy, Forces and Resources For a New Century," Project for the New American Century, *at* http://www.newamericancentury.org/publicationsreports.htm (Sept. 2000); *The National Security Strategy of the United States of America*, The White House, *at* http://www.whitehouse.gov/nsc/nss.pdf (Sept. 2002).

23. David Sanger, "Bush to Formalize a Defense Policy of Hitting First," *New York Times,* June 17, 2002, at A1.

24. Mark Matthews, "Bush to Issue 'Strike First' Strategy: Doctrine of Attacking Enemies Pre-Emptively Marks Major Policy Shift," *Baltimore Sun,* June 30, 2002, at A1. Armstrong, *supra* note 22.

25. Armstrong, supra note 22.

26. U.S. CONST. art. I, § 8.

27. Authorization for Use of Military Force against Iraq Resolution of 2002, Pub. L. No. 107-243, pmbl., 116 State. 1498 (2002).

28. *Id.* at §2.

29. *Id.* at §3.

30. *Id.* at §4.

31. U.N. CHARTER art. 51.

32. *Id.*

33. *See* discussion *supra* pp. 3-6.

34. The language originates in the text of the U.N. Charter, where the main purpose of the Security Council is to "restore international peace and security." *See generally,* United Nations Documentation Centre, *at* http://www.un.org/documents/, to read other UN Security Council resolutions.

35. Lobel & Ratner, *supra* note 9, at 126-27.

36. *Id.* at 125.

37. "The Situation Between Iraq and Kuwait," S.C. Res. 1441, U.N. SCOR, 58th Sess., 4644th mtg., para. 1, U.N. Doc. S/RES/1441 (2002).

38. *Id.* at para. 4.

39. *See, e.g.,* President George W. Bush, Remarks by the President on the United Nations Security Council Resolution, (Nov. 8, 2002), *at* http://www.whitehouse.gov/ news/releases/2002/11/20021108-1.html.

40. Don Kraus & Mark Epstein, "A War Avoided?," Campaign for U.N. Reform, *at* www.cunr.org/priorities/Iraq_analysis.htm (*last updated* Nov. 8, 2002).

41. Press Release, United Nations, "Security Council Holds Iraq in 'Material Breach' of Disarmament Obligations, Offers Final Chance to Comply, Unanimously Adoption Resolution 1441" (2002) (Nov. 8, 2002), *at* http://www.un.org/News/Press/docs/2002/SC7564.doc.htm.

42. Jeanne Whalen, "Russia Tries to Salvage Iraqi Oil Pacts," *Wall Street Journal,* Nov. 11, 2002, at A10.

43. Michael Moran & Alex Johnson, "Oil After Saddam: All Bets Are In," MSNBC News, *at* http://www.msnbc.com/ news/823985.asp (Nov. 7, 2002).

44. H.R. 86, 102nd Cong. (1991).

45. RESTATEMENT (THIRD) OF FOREIGN RELATIONS LAW OF THE UNITED STATES § 102, comment k (1987).

46. Jules Lobel, "The Limits of Constitutional Power: Conflicts Between Foreign Policy and International Law," 71 VA. L. REV. 1071 (1985).

47. *Letter dated 25 January 1999 from the Executive Chairman of the Special Commission established by the Secretary-General pursuant to paragraph 9(b)(i) of Security Council Resolution 687 (1991) addressed to the President of the Security Council,* U.N. SCOR, 54th Sess., Annex ¶ 8, U.N. Doc. S/1999/94 (1999), *available at* http://www.un.org/Depts/unscom/s99-94.htm.

48. 28 U.S.C. § 1350 (2002).

49. 28 U.S.C. § 1350 (2002)(note).

50. *Ashton et al v. Al Qaeda Islamic Army et al,* No. 02 CV-6977 (S.D.N.Y. filed Sept. 4, 2002); *Beyer et al v. Al Qaeda*

Islamic Army et al, No. 02 CV-6978 (S.D.N.Y. filed Sept. 4, 2002); *Burnett, St. v. Al Baraka Investment and Development, et al.* No. 02-CV-1616 (D.D.C. filed Aug 15, 2002).

51. Chomsky & Albert, *supra* note 1.
52. Phyllis Bennis, "U.S. Policy After Desert Fox," Arab-American Anti-Discrimination Committee Foreign Policy Symposium, *at* http://www.tni.org/archives/bennis/desert.htm (Dec. 29, 1998).
53. Chomsky & Albert, *supra* note 1.
54. Shalom & Albert, *supra* note 4.
55. Hans von Sponeck, "Iraq: Are There Alternatives to a Military Option?," American Friends Service Committee, *at* http:www.afsc.org/iraq/guide/alternatives.shtm (Dec. 9, 2001).
56. Steven R. Weisman, "A Nuclear North Korea: Diplomacy; Weighing 'Deterrence' vs. 'Aggression,'" *New York Times*, Oct. 18, 2002, at A8.
57. Lewis H. Lapham, "The Road to Babylon: Searching for Targets in Iraq," *Harper's Magazine*, Oct. 1, 2002.
58. Eric Schmitt, "U.S. Plan for Iraq Is Said to Include Attack on 3 Sides," *New York Times*, July 5, 2002, at A1.
59. "Iraq: Death of a Generation," *Arabic News* (Feb. 24, 2000), *at* http://www.arabicnews.com/ansub/Daily/Day/000224/2000022444.html.
60. The President's statement that Iraq has used "billions of dollars in illegal oil revenues to fund more weapons purchases rather than providing for the needs of the Iraqi people," is not true. According to a leading expert, Rahul Mahajan, author of *The New Crusade: America's War on Terrorism*, and the current U.N. Humanitarian Aid Coordinator in Iraq, "[m]oney that is received under the Oil for Food Program cannot be used for weapons purchases – all proceeds from such sales are deposited to an escrow account in New York which is controlled by the U.N. Sanctions Committee. The government of Iraq cannot touch this money." "Detailed Analysis of October 7 Speech," *supra* note 11.

61. *Background Information on Iraqi Sanctions*, Fellowship of Reconciliation, *at* http://www.forusa.org/Programs/Iraq/Sanctionsbkgrnd.html (*last visited* Nov. 18, 2002).

62. Human Rights Watch, "Needless Deaths in the Gulf War," Human Rights Watch, *at* http://www.hrw.org/reports/1991/gulfwar/index.htm#TopOfPage (1991).

63. Jane Salvage, *Collateral Damage: The Health and Environmental Costs of War on Iraq*, Medact, *at* www.medact.org/tbx/pages/sub.cfm?id=556 (Nov. 12, 2002).

64. Stephen Zunes, "Seven Reasons to Oppose a U.S. Invasion of Iraq," *FPIF Policy Report* (Aug. 2002), *at* http://www.fpif.org/papers/iraq2_body.html.

65. For example, 29.1% of the U.S. Army is African-American, as compared with 12% of the civilian work force, http://dod.mil/prhome/poprep2000/html/chapter3/chapter3_2.htm>. It is the Army which is likely to provide ground troops that will suffer the greatest number of casualties.

66. Steven R. Weisman, "Threats & Responses: The Risk to Israel," *New York Times*, Oct. 15, 2002, at A15.

67. *See* American Friends Service Committee, "Prevent Mass Expulsions Under Cover of War With Iraq" (Sept. 11, 2002) www.afsc.org/news/2002/stisrael.htm.

68. Don Van Natta Jr. & David Johnston, "Signs of Revived Qaeda Are Seen In Latest Strikes and New Tapes," *New York Times*, Oct. 13, 2002, at A1; Associated Press, *Text: Alleged Bin Laden Tape*, *at* http://www.washingtonpost.com/wp-dyn/articles/A44957-2002Nov12.html (Nov. 12, 2002). The tape quotes bin Laden saying: "As you kill, you get killed, and as you bomb, you get bombed."

69. Gary Fields et al., "As Death Toll Climbs in Bali, U.S. Debates Role of al Qaeda," *Wall Street Journal*, Oct. 14, 2002, at A1.

70. Thom Shanker & Eric Schmitt, "Reserve Call-Up For An Iraq War May Equal 1991's," *New York Times*, Oct. 28, 2002, at A1.

71. "Iraq," Energy Information Administration, *available at* http://www.eia.doe.gov/emeu/cabs/iraqfull.html (Dec. 1999).

72. Miriam Pemberton, "FPIF Talking Points: The Economic Costs of a War with Iraq," *Foreign Policy in Focus* (Sept. 13, 2002), *at* http://www.fpif.org/cgaa/talkingpoings/0209iraqwarcost_body.html.

73. *Congress: War Could Cost $9 Billion a Month*, USA Today (Oct. 1, 2002), *at* http://www.usatoday.com/news/washington/2002-10-01-iraq-costs-x.htm.

74. *See, e.g.,* Nancy Chang, *Silencing Political Dissent: How Post-September 11 Anti-Terrorism Measures Threaten Our Civil Liberties* (Seven Stories Press/Open Media Series: 2002); Michael Ratner, "Making Us Less Free: War on Terrorism or War on Liberty?" *at* www.humanrightsnow.org (May 1, 2002).

75. *Opportunism in the Face of Tragedy; Repression in the Name of Anti-terrorism*, Human Rights Watch, *at* http://www.hrw.org/campaigns/september11/opportunismwatch.htm (*last visited* Nov. 18, 2002).

76. *See* BBC article, Sunday, 1 December, 2002, "Australia Ready to Strike Abroad" at (http://news.bbc.co.uk/2/hi/asia-pacific/2532443.stm).

ABOUT THE AUTHORS

Michael Ratner is president of the Center for Constitutional Rights. Over the years, he has litigated a dozen cases challenging a U.S. president's authority to go to war, as well as many cases against international human rights violators resulting in millions of dollars in judgments. He acted as a principal counsel in the successful suit to close the camp for HIV-positive Haitian refugees on Guantanamo Base, Cuba. As part of the Center's focus on human rights and civil liberties violations in the wake of the September 11 attacks, he has led several cases representing detainees held at Camp X-ray in Cuba. Ratner also teaches international human rights litigation at Columbia Law School, and was formerly president of the National Lawyers Guild and a special counsel to Haitian president Jean-Bertrand Aristide to assist in the prosecution of human rights crimes. He is the author and co-author of several books and numerous articles including: Stephens and Ratner, *International Human Rights Litigation in U.S. Courts* (Transnational Publishers, Inc., 1996; Brody and Ratner, *The Pinochet Papers* (Kluwer 2000); Lobel and Ratner, *Bypassing the Security Council: Ambiguous Authorizations to Use Force, Cease Fires, and the Iraqi Inspection Regime,* 93 AJIL124 (January 1999). Among his many honors are: Trial Lawyer of the Year from the Trial Lawyers for Public Justice. See his web site: http://www.humanrightsnow.org.

Jennie Green, staff attorney at the Center for Constitutional Rights, specializes in international human rights legal actions, primarily lawsuits in U.S. courts against human rights violators. Recent cases include one against John Ashcroft and other U.S. government officials responsible for the post-9/11 arbitrary detention by the Immigration and Naturalization Service of thousands of non-citizens. Other successful cases have included those against Unocal, Royal Dutch/Shell, former Bosnian Serb leader Radovan Karadzic, former Chinese premier Li Peng, former Guatemalan minister of defense Hector Gramajo, Indonesian generals Johnny Lumintang and Sintong Panjaitan, Ethiopian police official Kelbessa Negewo, and former Haitian dictator Prosper Avril. She has also worked on international human rights claims in international fora such as the International Tribunals for the former Yugoslavia and Rwanda, the United Nations Commission on Human Rights, and the Inter-American human rights system. From 1992–1995, Green was the administrative director at the Harvard Law School Human Rights Program. She has worked for a wide range of nongovernmental human rights organizations, including Amnesty International, and currently serves on the advisory boards of numerous other organizations.

Barbara Olshansky is assistant legal director of the Center for Constitutional Rights. Her current docket at the Center includes class action lawsuits concerning immigrants' rights, prisoners' rights, race discrimination in employment, education, the environment and public health, and Native American rights. Olshansky graduated from Stanford Law School in 1985, and clerked for two years for Rose E. Bird, chief justice of the California Supreme Court. She is author of *Secret Trials and Executions: Military Tribunals and the Threat to Democracy* (Seven Stories Press/Open Media Series, 2002). She has also written several articles on democratic institutions, immigrants' rights, public access to radio programming and ownership, environmental racism, and a chapter on occupational exposures for the 2000 ABA treatise on environmental justice.

The Center for Constitutional Rights is a non-profit legal and educational organization dedicated to protecting and advancing the rights guaranteed by the United States Constitution and the Universal Declaration of Human Rights. CCR's work began in 1966 with the legal representation of civil rights activists in the Jim Crow South. Over the last four decades, CCR has played an important role in many popular movements for peace and social justice. CCR uses litigation proactively to combat government efforts to suppress political dissent, to advance the law in a positive direction, to empower poor communities and communities of color, to train the next generation of constitutional and human rights attorneys, and to strengthen the broader movement for constitutional and human rights.

The Center for Constitutional Rights condemns the Bush administration's rush to war against Iraq as an illegal, hypocritical, politically expedient, and dangerous misadventure. We believe that the new post-Cold War doctrine of "preventive strikes," which the President is using as the rationale to attack a sovereign nation and forcibly achieve a "regime change," is not only unconscionable but a violation of international law. In our judgment, rather than making the United States and the world more secure, the reckless course which Bush is pursuing is likely to increase insecurity and terrorism as peoples and nations, who already resent what they perceive to be a historical pattern of abuse of power by the U.S., lash out at a war that seems calculated to serve America's narrow economic interests rather than the cause of justice and peace. Moreover, the war against Iraq will consume billions of dollars at a time when the stock market is reeling from reports of corporate scandals and corruption and the lives of millions of working families in America are being devastated by an economy in crisis. Finally, we fear that Bush's strident call for war against Iraq is designed to produce a climate of "permanent emergency" where the people of our country will increasingly be asked (as is currently the case) to sacrifice civil liberties in the interest of defending the national interest.

Hence in this moment of national crisis, the Center for Constitutional Rights will remain true to its vision, values, and principles, vigorously promoting civil rights and human rights, social justice and social change, and the expansion of political and economic democracy as the best prescription for creating a just, humane, peaceful, and secure nation and world. Toward this end, we regard freedom of speech and the right to assemble peacefully without fear of harassment and intimidation by the government as an indispensable cornerstone of our democracy and a vital channel for the articulation of dissent. CCR will exercise its First Amendment rights toward the goals of defending our civil liberties and advancing the peaceful resolution of conflicts at this critical hour in our nation's history.

For information on our publications:
publications@ccr-ny.org

For information on how to contribute:
contributions@ccr-ny.org

CENTER FOR CONSTITUTIONAL RIGHTS
666 Broadway, 7th Floor
New York, NY 10012
(212) 614-6464 |www.ccr-ny.org

Open Media was founded in 1991 as a pamphlet publising effort in opposition to the Gulf War. Over the last 12 years, the Series has continued to publish a wide array of critically acclaimed scholars, activists, and artists committed to a common vision of "one world in which many worlds fit"—social justice, democracy, and human rights for all people.

"An operation out to change the world."
—THE NEW YORK TIMES

"Written by experts, they combine fact, analysis, and opinion in provocative packages that can be read in a single evening, leaving you with a sense of satisfaction about your understanding of an issue."
—UTNE READER

OTHER OPEN MEDIA TITLES

9-11
Noam Chomksy
$8.95 / ISBN: 1-58322-489-0

TERRORISM AND WAR
Howard Zinn with Anthony Arnove
$9.95 / ISBN: 1-58322-493-9

SECRET TRIALS AND EXECUTIONS: MILITARY
TRIBUNALS AND THE THREAT TO DEMOCRACY
Barbara Olshansky
$6.95 / ISBN:1-58322-437-4

OUR MEDIA, NOT THEIRS:
THE DEMOCRATIC STRUGGLE
AGAINST CORPORATE MEDIA
Robert W. McChesney & John Nichols
$9.95 / ISBN:1-58322-549-8

SILENCING POLITICAL DISSENT:
HOW POST-SEPT. 11 ANTI-TERRORISM MEASURES
THREATEN OUR CIVIL LIBERTIES
Nancy Chang
Foreword by Howard Zinn
$9.95 / ISBN: 1-58322-493-9

ISRAEL/PALESTINE:
HOW TO END THE WAR OF 1948
Tanya Reinhart
$11.95 / ISBN:1-58322-538-2

DEAD HEAT:
GLOBAL JUSTICE AND GLOBAL WARMING
Tom Athanasiou & Paul Baer
$9.95 / ISBN:1-58322-491-2

MEDIA CONTROL: THE SPECTACULAR
ACHIEVEMENTS OF PROPAGANDA. 2ND ED.
Noam Chomsky
$8.95 / ISBN: 1-58322-536-6

TERRORISM, THEIRS AND OURS
Eqbal Ahmad with David Barsamian
$6.95 / ISBN: 1-58322-490-4

SENT BY EARTH:
A MESSAGE FROM THE GRANDMOTHER SPIRIT
Alice Walker
$5.00 / ISBN: 1-58322-491-2

More Info: www.sevenstories.com

To order call: 800. 596 7437